SANDPLAY BRIDGES AND TRANSCENDENT FUNCTION

KATHERINE BRADWAY

The C.G. Jung Institute of San Francisco

Printed in the United States of America

Copies of this booklet are available from:
The C.G. Jung Institute of San Francisco
2040 Gough Street
San Francisco, California 94109

Katherine Bradway, Ph.D., a Jungian analyst in private practice in Mill Valley, California, is a Diplomate in Clinical Psychology of the American Board of Professional Psychology and a founding member of the C.G. Jung Institute of San Francisco.

The author wishes to express appreciation for the editorial assistance of John Beebe, M.D., Joan Alpert, and Barbara McClintock. She also wishes to acknowledge a grant from the Ernst and Eleanor van Loben Sels Scholarship Fund which made possible the presentation of the photographs in color.

SANDPLAY BRIDGES AND THE TRANSCENDENT FUNCTION*

"What is the point of Sandplay?" someone asked me at the end of a seminar series I had been giving. I do not recall my reply at that time. Now I would want to say that one of the essential points of sandplay is that it elicits a confrontation, and a bringing together, of opposite aspects or parts of oneself which leads to centering and the experiencing of wholeness. By providing the subject with a tray of sand, a source of water and a large selection of miniatures, with an invitation to "make anything you want to," the therapist supplies a "free and protected space" in which the subject can use the sand, water and objects to initiate and sustain a transforming process guided by the unconscious.

Dora Kalff, a Swiss analyst, studied with London's Margaret Lowenfeld who originated the method of the World Technique which Kalff then developed in connection with Jungian analysis. While using the technique, Kalff observed that the play in the sand progressed toward a union of opposites, and therefore gave her adaptation of the technique the name "Sandplay." Initial publications by Kalff and by Lowenfeld were followed by those of several of their students. Books that have been published on sandplay are included in the References given at the end.

---

*Based on a paper presented at a meeting of Sandplay Therapists in Zollikon, Switzerland, September 1982.

Many practitioners have remarked on the process of transformation, confirmed by clinical improvement, that the play in the sand reveals and seems to actually bring about. I think that a familiarity with what Jung has to say about the transcendent function may help to clarify the process of transformation observed in sandplay therapy, and may also throw light on the significance of some subjects' use of a special and important miniature in their sandplay: the bridge.

Jung refers to the transcendent function throughout his writings, but most of these references are brief except for an essay entitled "The Transcendent Function" which was written in 1916, but not published until 1957 when it appeared in *The Structure and Dynamics of the Psyche* (Vol. 8). Yet it was his discovery of this function that really showed him a way to heal the human conflicts that his years of work as a psychiatrist had revealed. In the transcendent function, Jung saw the psyche transcending its own deep divisions, which so often involve the claims of apparently irreconcilable opposites such as instinct and spirit, love and fear, dependency and independence.

Transcendent function is the term that Jung uses for a process through which such opposites are united. The transcendent function mediates between the warring opposites and unites them with a reconciling symbol, which is experienced consciously as a new attitude transcending the original divided state of the self. The prototype of opposites is contained in the relationship between the conscious and the unconscious since emotionally significant content in the one is countered by its opposite in the other. The transcendent function begins with a confrontation between the opposites in the conscious and unconscious, leading to a collaboration of conscious and unconscious data which effects a transition from the old attitude to a new, more comprehensive one. It is often only through a change in attitude that we can effectively change our behavior in a natural and stable way. Later

Jung would say that conflicts are not so much solved as outgrown.

Jung notes that "function" as used in "transcendent function" is not to be understood as a basic function of the conscious or unconscious, but rather as a complex function made up of other functions; and further, that "transcendent" does not denote a metaphysical quality but merely indicates the fact that this function facilitates the *transition* from one attitude to another. The new attitude transcends the conflicts implicit in the old, though the new attitude may well lead to a fresh opposition with the unconscious to be overcome by a further activity of the transcendent function. Jung points out that the progressive uniting of opposites is part of the process of individuation. "Psychology has no proof that this process does not unfold itself at the instigation of God's will."

Jung is really suggesting that what is required to develop the transcendent function is first and foremost an active unconscious. He observes that the most readily accessible expressions of the unconscious are dreams. After stating why dreams are difficult to use in developing the transcendent function, Jung refers to the value of drawing or painting and working with plastic materials. He emphasizes that it is not important for the product to be technically correct or aesthetically satisfying, but merely for the fantasy to have free play so that a product is created which is influenced by both conscious and unconscious, embodying, as he says, "the striving of the unconscious for the light and the striving of the conscious for substance." At the time of making these observations (1916), Jung was not familiar with sandplay as used today. Apparently his first encounter with it was in its form as the World Technique, presented by Lowenfeld at a 1937 conference in London. But the grown-up Jung had done his own playing in the sand on the shores of Lake Zurich in 1912 as he describes in *Memories, Dreams, Reflections*. He discovered that using sand and carefully selected stones to build miniature structures — finally "a whole village" — helped him to connect with unconscious contents and to accept their regulating counteraction to his conscious thoughts.

In his essay "The Transcendent Function," Jung says that there are two main tendencies or ways of dealing with material obtained through this dialectical process. The two ways are the way of artistic formulation and the way of understanding. Jung points out that both tendencies have dangers: "The danger of the aesthetic tendency is an overvaluation of the formal 'artistic' worth of the fantasy productions; the libido is diverted from the real goal of the transcendent function and sidetracked into purely aesthetic problems of artistic expression. The danger of wanting to understand the meaning is overvaluation of the content, which is subjected to intellectual analysis and interpretation, so that the essential symbolic character of the product is lost." In the use of sandplay, both of these tendencies — and potentials for danger — occur. Jung perceives the two tendencies as bound together in a compensatory relationship. He elucidates, " . . . aesthetic formulation needs understanding of the meaning, and understanding needs aesthetic formulation." Sandplay avoids verbal solutions by asking the subject to use the hands rather than verbal speech to develop the fantasy production. As Jung says later in the same essay: "Often the hands know how to solve a riddle with which the intellect has wrestled in vain."

Sandplay seems to be a special opportunity for the natural and spontaneous phenomenon of the transcendent function to occur. The therapist's role is to recognize the phenomenon and honor it. I think there are three ways that sandplay encourages the development of the transcendent function. I will name them and then discuss them:

1. A sandplay scene is a product of the unconscious and the conscious.

2. Sandplay is conducive to the "synchronistic moment."

3. Sandplay provides for a presentation of, confrontation between, and uniting of opposites.

Sandplay as *a product of the unconscious as well as of the conscious* is exemplified in a comparison of two consecutive sand scenes made by a man whom I will call Sam. Sam's first sandtray, shown at the top of page 6 includes a dinosaur which he sees as the bad or evil part of himself. The priest (Sam is Catholic) represents the judging part of himself. The cannon aimed at the dinosaur is the part of himself that is trying to destroy the evil part.

In Sam's second sandtray, shown at the bottom of page 6, another dinosaur is in approximately the same location as the previous one. The authority figure at the top has become a king instead of a priest, suggesting the constellation of the Self. An owl has replaced the cannon. The mermaid is a new introduction. Sam commented, "I guess the owl is the wise part of me wanting to deal with evil (dinosaur). But I am attracted to the Siren mermaid."

The remarkable feature about these two sand scenes is that the second was made ten years after the first, with Sam's having no conscious memory of having made the previous sand scene. I too had forgotten the making of the first scene and only discovered it when I filed the notes and picture of the second one.

Sam had terminated analysis a few months after making the initial sandtray and had been functioning satisfactorily until he became enchanted with a woman in his office where he worked, leading to an obsession similar to the one from which he had recovered ten years earlier. Because Sam experienced happiness in his marriage, the debilitating obsession was extremely painful to him. He reentered analysis and soon after starting, made the second sand scene. The use of wisdom has been substituted for shooting. The authority of the priest has been integrated as the authority of the Self. A significant addition is the presence of the anima, in the form of the mermaid, the tempting pixie. She is in the center of things, suggesting her central role in his psychological life at

Sam: First sandtray

Sam: Second sandtray

this time. My purpose in presenting Sam's two sandtrays is to illustrate the way in which a sandplay image (the dinosaur) is preserved in the unconscious and forms a pattern for a subsequent sandtray production — in this instance after a period of ten years with no conscious memory. The comparison confirms that sandplay is a product of the unconscious as well as of the conscious.

The occurrence that Kalff refers to as the *synchronistic moment* is a second way sandplay helps in the development of the transcendent function. Kalff explains what the term means to her as follows: "The presentation of the unconscious by the patient in the sandtray and the simultaneous recognition of it as such by the therapist provides the link between the unconscious of one and the conscious of the other and is the synchronistic moment that is healing to the patient." (This is analogous to Jung's discussion of the "actual moment" in his writings on psychotherapy.) At such a moment of deep sharing of an emergent attitude, the therapist may often make no vocal comment. In Kalff's book on sandplay, she refers to an instance in which she simply puts her arm around little Marina to show she understands.

Or the therapist may make some brief vocalization of recognition, such as "Ah yes." Or the therapist may ask a question that furthers or deepens what is occurring. For example, at another point in her sandplay with Marina, Kalff asks her what a figure is doing in the woods. This elicits Marina's reply: "He has to bring the light into the dark forest," to which Kalff agrees.

I think what Kalff says next in writing about this fragment of psychotherapy is of particular importance because it reflects the combination of intellect and feeling on the part of the therapist. Kalff writes "I knew that her psyche had started on the healing path, and I was greatly touched by this." Dora Kalff was not only knowing with her mind but was appreciating with her heart. I believe this combination is an essential feature of sandplay therapy. Kalff further adds in reference to the healing path which Marina has started: "Only through the dark does the path lead to the light. An eternal truth was expressed here, spontaneously, coming from the unconscious of the child."

Although Jung does not include this kind of interchange in his more intellectual discussion of the transcendent function, for me it is an extension of the phenomenon that Jung discovered. And in this example, it was the uniting of the opposites of light and dark that symbolized the bringing together of the conscious and unconscious.

A third way in which sandplay helps the transcendent function to occur is by its *providing a physical space for the presentation and uniting of opposites.* The left and right sides of the tray, the far and near halves of the tray (top and bottom in pictures), and the two diagonals provide opposing sites for placing objects or sets of objects which represent conflicting opposites. What is placed between the opposites or the succession of scenes, or sometimes — particularly with children — a movement within the sandtray provides for a bringing together of the opposites. We can then speak of the opposites as having been bridged. This important event may be represented by an actual bridge or it may be expressed by other means: a path, a river, even the looking of a figure from one section to a figure or object in the opposite section or, as shown in Sam's tray, a shooting — any way that the two sides or sections are made to be dynamically connected with one another.

A bridge is a readily observed expression of the connection. The placing of the bridge is the actual attempt to connect what is symbolized or represented on the two sides of the bridge; it is not just the potential for making the connection. Sandplay is a dynamic happening, not a static production. The bridge provides for the phenomenon of the transcendent function as described by Jung.

Examples of this process are contained in comparisons of pairs of consecutive scenes made by three different men in which the first of the pair of scenes includes a bridge and the next following scene indicates a resulting transformation. Photographs of these three pairs of sandplay scenes appear on pages 11, 13 and 16 with the first tray of each pair at the top and the second tray at the bottom of the page.

The three men who produced these trays were college graduates in their 40's who had been raised in traditional, unbroken homes of top socio-economic status. All three were having problems in their relationships with women: Hal was being left by his wife; Carl was leaving his wife; Jim had never been able to relate sexually to any woman (or man) even though he had been attracted to several women. Both Hal and Carl had made many sandtrays prior to making the pair of consecutive trays to be discussed here. For Jim, it was a new experience.

In Hal's first sandtray (top of page 11) a stream extends from a tree at top center, with two huge worms on it, to three lily pads at bottom left. On the right of the stream is a gorilla and a blue horse; on the left are two arms coming out of the sand. After using the ladder as a bridge across the stream, Hal said "I need something small to be inching its way across," and placed a nude boy on the "bridge." He added "I see the hands as the feminine buried in my unconscious — ominous. I couldn't cross where the hands are — too close to the primeval — it would be overwhelming. To cross here made sense." He made no mention of the horse or gorilla. In this tray a connection between Hal's masculine spirit (blue horse and gorilla) and a buried anima seems to be in process. The worms on the tree might be threatening to new growth. Whether they are larvae which will develop into butterflies or moths, thus symbolizing transformative energy, was not determined.

Hal's second tray of the pair (bottom of page 11) contains a centered round pool of water into which he dropped blue paint to color it. The lower point of an inverted triangle of objects is made up of a clay pot (feminine symbol) containing water and two pieces of turquoise, balanced by a fanciful animal head. Regarding the attachment of the scorpion to the gorilla, above and to the left of the pool, Hal said "The gorilla represents known overt aggression; the scorpion represents unknowable hidden power." This shows an integrating of masculine and feminine strength. The black and white stone is also a combination of opposites. Access to the unconscious is suggested by the multiple representations of water: pool, pot of water, a Zodiacal water sign (Scorpio). Something sacred or spiritual is indicated by placing turquoise in the pot and by making the water in the pool blue. The connection between masculine and feminine that was being attempted by the bridge in the previous tray is now accomplished as a true union of opposites in this scene, with

Hal: First sandtray

Hal: Second sandtray

the probable achievement of a new attitude in Hal. Growth in this scene consists of several unburdened trees.

Hal showed marked satisfaction with his second tray: "I wanted to break new ground and I think I have." It was a couple of years later when Hal was reviewing his course of development in preparation for terminating analysis that he referred to this time in his life as being the time when the most significant inner and outer changes occurred.

Carl's two sandtrays (page 13) also show movement from the first tray to the second. Carl made a mound at the top left of the first tray and placed on it a black figure in robes surrounded by a half circle consisting of a fruit tree, a bonfire, a stalk of three roses, a boy playing a flute and another bonfire. The features of this corner give the impression of spiritual or religious energy. On the other side of the stream is the work-a-day world: men and women working on a farm.

Carl made no comment regarding the two women at the bridge at left center, one carrying a baby about to cross the bridge and one carrying a water jug coming off of it. Baby and water carrying are traditional feminine activities. In retrospect I see the two women as the feminine participating in the making of a connection between the spiritual and the temporal spheres. The red carriage drawn by four white horses at bottom left must represent "the journey," but it is separated from both the spiritual and the temporal areas by water with no bridge for passage.

Among the last items Carl placed was an Eskimo with a gun which he positioned in many ways: "I can't decide where I want it to go." I asked if the gun was aimed at anyone. "It's aimed across the bridge." And then as if to counter-

Carl: First sandtray

Carl: Second sandtray

act destruction he placed a shepherd and house on the far right of the tray, the former a protector of animals and the latter a protector of people. Finally he placed a skull on top of the carriage, but almost immediately removed it. Perhaps he had an indecisive sense that something had to die to foster forward movement. He said, "That's enough — it's about right."

In this tray there is an attempt to connect or reconcile religious, sacred, spiritual concerns with the demands of temporal, work-a-day achievement. Carl's anima, or inner feminine, wants to help in making the connection; his aggressive side is struggling in its ambivalence toward making the connection. But the connection, the bridge, remains in position.

In Carl's second sandtray there is, as in Hal's second tray, a centered pool. In Carl's pool appears a mermaid. As in Sam's second tray, the anima is in the center of things. A huge shell at bottom center emphasizes the feminine. The working world, including athletic performers, appears displaced to the far right, and the spiritual aspects are represented at the top by temples and a Greek goddess. Regarding the reappearance in right center of the flute player, which must be connected with feeling, Carl remarked, "I identify with him the most." This tray also includes a bridge, but the area to the left of the bridge contains only a single object: a female torso at the bottom left corner. Toward it an Eskimo is directing a spear. There is still ambivalence toward the feminine, which is creating energy. A connection is being made using this energy. Carl was deeply moved in viewing and discussing these trays several years later. His extraverted nature had necessitated his living out some of the ambivalence depicted in these scenes before an outer transformation was fully realized.

Although Jim had been in analysis for several years, he had never shown an interest in making a sandtray until one day he came in for his appointment and announced that he would like to try his hand at it. His first sandtray (page 16) is less well defined as to opposites than are the first sandtrays of the other two men. To the left of the bridge there is a walrus, a dried tree, pieces of wood and stones and coral. To the right there is a well, a house with a dog in front of it, a green tree and a cow drinking from a trough. Large rocks and a piece of driftwood were placed in three corners and a miniature garden pool in the lower center. A second well is in nearly the exact center. A fence along the right side is described as being "Between where one is living and the outside world." His inner world needs protection. Early in the making of the scene, Jim placed an egg in the right lower corner but removed it before the scene was completed. No human figures are included. Jim described the whole as being a vacation cabin at the beach, and yet he made no attempt to move the sand to utilize the blue base of the tray for representing water, a possibility he had been shown before making the tray. Even the bridge spans a dry trough. The bridge is joining a land area on the right that has implied connections with water below the ground (two wells and miniature garden pool) and a water area on the left that has dried plant life. Each side represents both dry and wet, both aridity and life-giving moisture. The leafless dry plant bespeaks lack of rain or sky (father) water. The sources of water on the right indicate earth (mother) water. His father had died a few years before; his mother was still alive. I feel (or rather intuit in a manner than I don't fully understand) that this scene reflects Jim's attempt to reconcile dependence-independence conflicts. He has a need for both independence and dependence in the receiving of life's (emotional) nourishment. One of the three animals, the cow, is supplied with water to drink.

Jim: First sandtray

Jim: Second sandtray

Jim's second sandtray (page 16) consists of a centering, this time in the form of a mound rather than the pool appearing in the other two second sandtrays. On the top of the mound is a gorilla with many animals "coming up to challenge this guy." Water is depicted at the right where water birds, which connect sky, earth, and water by being able to live and move in all three realms, are coming to drink and nourish themselves. Masculine and feminine values (physical strength; provision of nourishment) are differentiated, but are in juxtaposition to one another. They are not united as they were in Hal's second sandtray.

At the next appointment, a week later, Jim told me that he had been able to have sexual intercourse with the woman whom he had been dating for the past few months. This was his first full sexual experience — at the age of 49. He asked, "Do you think it was the sandtray I did last time that let me do that?" In the sandtray he made at this session (not reproduced here) he started by putting an egg in the exact center of the tray, and let it remain there. He added a frog with a baby frog on its back, and included humans for the first time: Indians travelling in a canoe. This scene showed flowing and new life. A few months later Jim's long-time dependency on me was significantly decreased and he was able to make a successful transfer to a male analyst. (It is this kind of experience that makes me think that sandplay is not just a medium of exchanges between the patient and me, but is a healing vehicle in its own right, like dreams.)

To summarize the pairs of sandtrays of three men using a bridge in the first of two consecutive trays: In all three instances the presentation of a bridge in one sandtray was followed by a sandtray in which a clear-cut centering appeared and in which a relationship between, or a differentiation between, the masculine and feminine was represented. Hal and Carl were at a point in their development where they needed to focus on the anima. At his level of development, Jim required a differentiation of the masculine from the maternal, nourishing feminine. For all three men, regardless of their stage of development, an experiencing of masculine strength and power was important. For Hal this was expressed as an integration with feminine strength. For Carl masculinity was expressed in opposition to the feminine, at the same time that connection was being made between the spiritual and the temporal achieving spheres. For Jim masculine strength was expressed as a differentiation from the feminine, following an apparent attempt to reconcile his conflicting needs for independence and dependency. How this transformation manifested in their outer lives varied. Jim's was the most dramatic. Carl's was the most subtle and not consciously appreciated until some years later. Hal's was experienced as a breakthrough at the time of the making of the second tray and anticipated steady subsequent development. For all three men, a tray evidencing development of the transcendent function followed a tray in which a bridge uniting opposites appeared in the sand. Each man's second tray showed a process of centering and transformation, demonstrating that sandplay had given him a symbolic means for connecting opposing parts of himself. At this time each man experienced a new wholeness.

REFERENCES

Dundas, Evalyn. *Symbols Come Alive in the Sand.* Privately printed, 1978.

Jung, Carl Gustav. *Memories, Dreams, Reflections.* New York: Pantheon Books, 1961.

________ *Psychological Types.* Collected Works, vol. 6. Princeton: Princeton University Press, 1971.

________ *Structure and Dynamics of the Psyche.* Collected Works, vol. 8. 2nd ed. Princeton: Princeton University Press, 1969.

________ *The Symbolic Life.* Collected Works, vol. 18. Princeton: Princeton University Press, 1950.

Kalff, Dora M. *Sandplay, A Psychotherapeutic Approach to the Psyche.* Santa Monica: Sigo Press, 1980. A revision with a new translation of *Sandplay; Mirror of a Child's Psyche.* San Francisco: Browser Press, 1971.

Lowenfeld, Margaret. *The World Technique.* London: George Allen and Unwin, 1979.

Sandplay Studies; Origins, Theory and Practice. San Francisco, C.G. Jung Institute of San Francisco, 1981. Consists of chapters by Katherine Bradway, Karen Signell, Geraldine Spare, Charles Stewart, Louis Stewart, and Clare Thompson.

Weinrib, Estelle. *Images of the Self; The Sandplay Therapy Process.* Boston: Sigo Press, 1983.